T0015999

THE

GHOSTLY TALES

OF

MYSTIC

Published by Arcadia Children's Books
A Division of Arcadia Publishing
Charleston, SC
www.arcadiapublishing.com

Spooky America is a trademark of Arcadia Publishing, Inc.

First published 2023

Manufactured in the United States

ISBN: 978-1-4671-9726-7

Library of Congress Control Number: 2023931837

All images used courtesy of Shutterstock.com; p. 2 Faina Gurevich/Shutterstock.com;
pp. 32-33 James Kirkikis/Shutterstock.com; p. 102 Spiroview Inc/Shutterstock.com;
pp. 98-99 Enrico Della Pietra/Shutterstock.com.

Notice: The information in this book is true and complete to the best of our
knowledge. It is offered without guarantee on the part of the author or Arcadia
Publishing. The author and Arcadia Publishing disclaim all liability in connection with
the use of this book.

Spooky America

THE
GHOSTLY TALES
OF
MYSTIC

BETH LANDIS HESTER

Adapted from *Haunted Mystic* by Courtney McInvale

arcadia
CHILDREN'S BOOKS

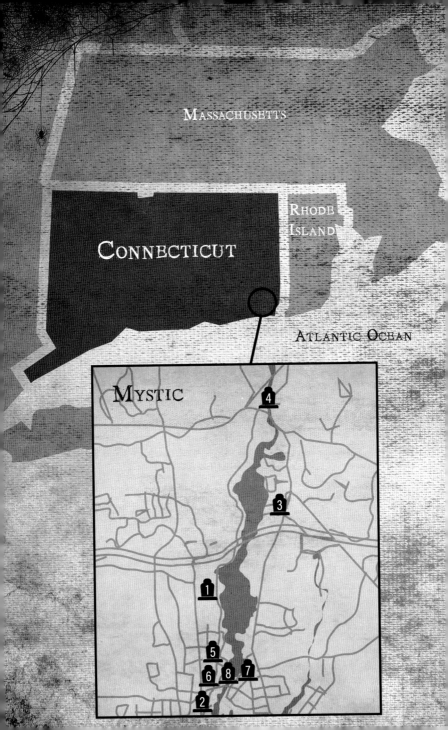

MASSACHUSETTS

RHODE ISLAND

CONNECTICUT

ATLANTIC OCEAN

MYSTIC

Table of Contents & Map Key

Mystic Seaport

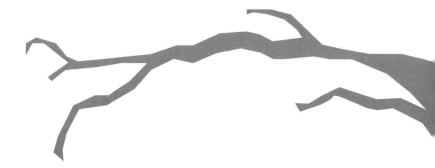

Welcome to
Spooky Mystic!

In the charming coastal village of Mystic, Connecticut, the past isn't just in history books. A historical district called Mystic Seaport—filled with restored ships, historic buildings, old-fashioned shops, and people dressed in period costumes—lets visitors experience what this New England seaport was like almost four hundred years ago. Of course, old ships and costumes aren't the only things from the past you'll find in Mystic. This town has a unique—some might even say *ghostly*—connection to the people who have shaped it through the centuries. For better or worse, the spirits of Mystic are still making their presence known in spooky and mysterious ways.

A relationship to the water has always defined Mystic. The Mystic River, Long Island Sound, and Atlantic Ocean have been the source of jobs, food, and opportunity. But Mystic is also a place of tragedy, mystery, and danger. Those uneasy feelings can lead the imagination to dark places—spooky stories, hauntings, and more.

Read on to learn about local legends, mischievous ghosts, restless souls, and a fiery curse that burned for hundreds of years (and might just be smoldering still). Then decide for yourself: How much is *truly* mystical in Mystic?

CHAPTER 1

A Burning Legacy

SINCE 1637

"*This is the place!*" When Dutch and English settlers first saw Mystic, they must have been excited. After all, the weather was moderate compared to other parts of New England. The land provided for good hunting and farming. The river offered a safe and spacious harbor for boat building. It was a perfect place for shipping and receiving supplies. Good weather, good food, good business, safe harbor—what more could you ask for?

The Europeans weren't the first to notice the value of this land. The Pequot, Narragansett, and Mohegan peoples had long hunted, fished, and farmed here. In fact, they frequently went to battle against each other to hold on to it. It was the Pequots who reigned supreme when the new settlers arrived at Mystic. They were wealthy, skilled, and victorious in war. They were masterful at hunting in the wooded hills, and fishing in the waterway they called *missi-tuk* (which means "wide, wind-blown river"). They were

successful traders, and, at least for a while, had peaceful relationships with their European neighbors. They were also lucky. An early epidemic of smallpox swept the region and killed many. But it largely spared the Pequots in their fortified villages.

Then, in the 1630s, the Pequots' luck changed. A second wave of smallpox killed around eighty percent of their population. Their territory shrank. Trading relationships soured. The settlers had begun demanding costly fines for traded goods—more than the

Pequots could pay. Skirmishes with the British created a tense atmosphere. It seemed like the tension might explode at any moment. And then, it did. Several local Englishmen died

in what was probably a series of accidents. But the settlers blamed the Pequots.

The British struck back at their former friends in brutal fashion. With the help of the Narragansetts and Mohegans, the English leader Captain John Mason led a nighttime attack on the Pequots. The main Pequot village was set atop a hill. It was surrounded by a wall of upright logs. Inside the walls, families lived in round, bark-covered wigwam homes.

One night, as the Pequots lay sleeping, John Mason ordered his soldiers to set the village on fire. In no time, screams and smoke filled the air. The flames quickly spread through the wooden structures. With the village gates blocked by Mason's troops, hundreds of people burned inside the log walls. Those who managed to escape faced gunshots. Pequots from other villages rushed to help. But by the time the sun was up, all but a handful were dead.

Mason bragged about the massacre. In his journal he wrote, "And thus in little more than an Hour's space was their impregnable Fort with themselves utterly Destroyed, to the Number of six or seven Hundred, as some of themselves confessed. There were only seven taken Captive and about seven escaped."

Mason justified the attack by describing the Pequots as dangerous savages. Even at the time, though, his actions were shocking to many—including the Narragansetts and Mohegans. The British had claimed the land, but at a terrible cost . . . one that some say still haunts Mystic to this day.

Over the years, the British settlement at Mystic (from the Pequot name *missi-tuk*) grew and became a town. Stores, hotels, and homes were built. The everyday patterns of a community took shape within their walls: shopping, meeting, learning, praying. But as the decades passed, there was another pattern that was hard to ignore: Mystic seemed to have an unusual—even suspicious—number of fires.

The Denisons were one of the first families to settle in Mystic. In 1717, their home burned to the ground on the wedding night of a family member. Other locations nearby have experienced multiple fires. Near Mystic's famous drawbridge, there's a now-empty lot that was once home to a theater, office building, "political pulpit," and even a roller-skating rink. Each was destroyed by fire in the years 1863, 1880, 1910, 2000. At East Main and Cottrell Street, a large meeting house burned in 1885 and was rebuilt as an opera house. It burned in 1900 and later reopened as a movie theater. It burned *again* in 1960, in a fire that destroyed the theater AND eight businesses surrounding it! Even Mystic's firehouse burned at least three times before it moved to a new location.

You may be tempted to try to explain away these events, especially in a town as old as Mystic! But consider this: All these fires were reported as suspicious or likely intentionally set. And yet, to this day, authorities have not been able to identify a single suspect. The fires took place many years apart, sometimes even affecting different buildings on the same site. They seem to return to their "homes" again and again. In fact, a massive four-alarm fire destroyed parts of Mystic's historic Seaport Marine in the fall of 2022. The fires tend not to hurt people, only property. But the cost of repairs is usually more than the owners can pay. And the fires almost always occur right around dawn—just about when John Mason's troops set fire to the Pequot's hilltop village.

We may never know the truth behind Mystic's burning legacy, but one thing feels certain: This terrible act seems to have invited the curse that still smolders in Mystic today.

Captain Daniel Packer Inne

BUILT 1756

These days, you can leave New York by car at lunchtime and be in Boston in time for dinner. But in the 1700s, the journey took two days in a horse and carriage. People needed a place to have a meal and spend the night along the way. Mystic's Captain Daniel Packer Inne had everything a tired and hungry traveler could ask for: a convenient location about halfway between the two cities, delicious food, and the warm hospitality of Captain Packer himself.

Daniel Packer was a captain twice over: a captain of the sea as the master of a square-rigged sailing ship, and a captain in the army during the American Revolution. He loved entertaining his guests with stories about his days at sea and his wartime adventures. He would happily chat away as he showed them to their rooms, pointing out the view of the river and harbor before he wished them a good night.

The next morning over breakfast, he might tell them about the time a traveling circus came to stay. There were no bridges in town yet, so he would load guests, carriages, and horses onto his rope ferry, telling his passengers about meeting George Washington during the war as he pulled the barge, hand over hand, along the rope that spanned the Mystic River from west to east.

Between the steady flow of guests and his own large family (including his wife, Hanna, and seven children), the house was always bustling with energy and things to do. Captain Packer loved it all. He even mused that he would never leave, staying in the house forever to watch over it. But surely that was just the good-natured Captain Packer spinning another tale ... right?

Captain Daniel Packer was just the first in a long line of Captain Packers. About a century later, Charles Carroll Packer came along. He was Daniel's great-grandson. Charles and his wife, Fanny, filled the house on Water Street with the cheerful noise of a young family.

Charles carried on his great-grandfather's legacy of ship captaining and hospitality. He and Fanny made their home a friendly place that was a comfort to visitors and friends in need. This was especially true for Fanny's sister "Muddie" Morse Clift and her young daughter, Ada. After the death of her husband, Captain Clift, Muddie couldn't bear to remain in the family's home without him. She and Ada moved in with the Packers. Seven-year-old Ada was delighted. Instead of an empty house in mourning, she was now surrounded by fun-loving cousins. They could frequently be heard giggling in the hallways. Sadly, her joy was short-lived: Ada died of scarlet fever before her eighth birthday.

Another century passed. Family members still lived in the house. But it had become so run-down and difficult to manage that they decided to sell it. One group of potential buyers wanted to knock it down and build modern apartments. But Richard and Lulu Kiley saw something special beneath the shabby surface. In 1979, the Kileys bought it and set to work restoring it. Not long after, the couple had their first sign of something a little spooky at 32 Water Street.

One day, as the couple worked on the house, an elderly woman approached them in a huff and said sternly, "I am a direct descendent of Captain Daniel Packer. He came to me in a dream last night, and he is *not happy* about what is happening to his house!"

The Kileys were surprised. They told the woman that they felt confident she would like the end results of the renovation. But the woman stalked off unconvinced. How strange! The woman and Captain Packer needn't have worried. Over the next four years, Richard and Lulu attended to every detail. They even used construction techniques from the 1700s to restore the fireplaces, mantles, and beams to their original glory. The house was updated in the most authentic way. Captain Packer would have been delighted with how they planned to use the space, too. They had decided to open a fine-dining restaurant and event space where people could enjoy good food and good company. Just the way the captain had hosted guests centuries before.

When at last the building was ready, the

woman returned. With the same strange, stern manner, she announced, "You will not be seeing me again. The captain came to me in my dreams last night and said he is quite pleased with what you've done with the place. It looks perfect, and he will be looking in on it." Then off she went, leaving the couple mystified—but also glad that they had her approval, and maybe even Captain Packer's as well!

If the Kileys were skeptical of the captain's intentions at first, it didn't last long. People began to report seeing a sea captain appear, then suddenly disappear. In some rooms, fireplaces appeared to be tended by an invisible hand. Was this Daniel Packer "looking in?" Were the ghostly sounds of boots stomping and doors slamming signs that the captain was keeping busy, even when the building was empty? One thing seemed certain: Something unseen was watching over the restaurant and protecting it from one of Mystic's greatest dangers: *fire*.

One evening, a night manager noticed a

burning smell in the bar area. She tracked it to a small plume of smoke rising from a frayed electrical wire. The night manager knew that this could become a dangerous situation if the damaged wire stayed connected to a power source. So she went to the electrical panel and switched off the power to the corresponding appliance. Then she gathered her things and walked toward the door to head home.

But to her surprise, she couldn't get through the door! It was like an unseen hand was pushing her back, keeping her in the room. Understandably upset, the manager called the owners to help. By the time Richard joined the manager in the restaurant, both could smell that the smoke had not actually gone away at all. In fact, it was getting stronger. They searched for the source. They found the same frayed wire, now red hot! The wrong switch had been flipped in the electrical panel. If the manager hadn't been stopped at the door, the whole building could have burned down. Could that have been Daniel Packer doing all he could to keep his home—and the people inside it—safe?

Another manager had a similar experience with the ghost guiding his path. His routine for leaving the bar each night was always the same: latch the back door from the inside, then walk out the front door to go home, locking it behind him. Every single night . . . until this one.

The manager locked the back door from the inside as usual, then walked toward the front door to leave. Like the other manager, though, he just couldn't seem to do it! The odd force stopped him from going his usual way. But he also felt it encouraging him to do the opposite—go back in. *Okay,* he thought. *I'll go out the back door instead.* When he did, he saw a fire in the dumpster behind the building! He called the fire department, who arrived in a hurry and put out the flames before they could spread.

While Captain Packer works to keep a careful eye on things, there is another spirit at 32 Water Street who seems to be all about playtime. You may spot her bouncing a ball in a stairwell, standing near a fireplace, giggling as she peeks into a bathroom, or looking out of a third-floor window as ships sail by on the Mystic River. She seems so full of life. Those

who see her think she is an ordinary child, though a little old-fashioned-looking. These eyewitnesses often ask the staff her name, how old she is, and who her parents are. Staff members have learned to simply brush off their questions with a smile. It's far easier than explaining, "Oh, that's Ada. She is seven years old ... *and has been dead since 1874.*"

Playful Ada is known to enjoy hide-and-seek. It is pretty hard to beat her hiding skills! Richard and Lulu's daughter Allie is the current manager of the inn. One day, she was sitting at one of the dining tables with a friend. The friend's eight-year-old daughter was playing happily nearby. The two women heard the girl laughing and chatting, though no one else was there. After a while, the girl asked for help in finding her playmate. "I can hear her, but I can't see her," she explained. "She says her name is Ada."

A descendant of the Packer family who

knew all about Ada went looking for her one day. He told a friend about his plan to find her in the restaurant. He would search in her favorite places, call her by name, maybe even sing a Christmas carol (she was said to love them no matter the time of year). The friend wished him luck, but after hours of searching, Ada's cousin could not find the girl anywhere. He checked the second-story stairwell, the fireplaces, the bathrooms. He whispered her name aloud. But Ada never appeared. At last, he gave up. He went home, called his friend with the disappointing report, and went to bed defeated.

Later that night, however, he was awoken by a tugging at his toes. To his shock, when he opened his eyes, a young child was standing by his bed! Dark hair, dark eyes, an old-fashioned dress, and a joyful giggle as she ran off—it was *Ada*! When he called his friend the next morning to tell him, the friend said he already knew. "She came here, too!" he exclaimed. "Ada wanted me to assure you it was her." When Ada wants to be found, she is found—or finds you!

If you find yourself walking by the inn, look to the top-floor window. Perhaps you'll see a young girl's face there, watching the boats on the river. Send a salute toward the captain if you see him. And know the home the Packer family loved is being well cared for by the Kileys—including Allie, who finishes each workday with a warm, "Goodnight, Ada. Goodnight, Captain. I'll see you tomorrow."

Mystic Seaport

Whitehall Mansion

BUILT 1771

By today's standards, "mansion" may seem like too grand a name for this family-home-turned-inn. But when it was built around 250 years ago, the home of Sarah and Dr. Dudley Woodbridge was considered grand, indeed. Whitehall was the home of the couple and their nine children. It also served as Dr. Dudley's medical office. Over time, the children moved away to start their own families—all except Lucy, who never married, and Benjamin, who died of an illness at the age of twelve. In fact, some believe these two still haven't left to this day.

The mansion now operates as part of the hotel across the road, offering a quirky (and spooky) alternative to the main hotel's modern rooms. Guests are surrounded by antique furnishings as they walk across the wide-plank floors to rooms named after the Woodbridge

family. But when they encounter the haunted happenings there, some of them walk—or even run—right back to the hotel across the street! Even those brave enough to stay the night report a strong sensation of being watched. Sometimes they turn around the family portraits on the walls just to make *sure* there aren't any faces looking at them. Three of the rooms, named for Lucy, Benjamin, and Betsey, are thought to be especially haunted.

In Betsey's room, a door leads up to an attic. Some think this part of the house was used as a safe space for enslaved people seeking freedom on the Underground Railroad. You can only imagine how fearful of capture they must have felt, and how anxious they must have been to reach their destination. It's possible those feelings have lingered in Betsey's room ever since. That's just the kind of uneasy energy guests report after staying in this room.

Though the door to the attic is locked, people say it seems poised to open at any moment. There's an eerie sense that people are still hiding right behind it, nervously preparing for the next part of their journey north toward Canada.

Benjamin's room, on the other hand, holds somber feelings of loss and sadness. Thought to be the room where the twelve-year-old boy died all those years ago, some guests feel a tug on the sheets or a general feeling of being watched. Could it be that Benjamin is still there? Some rule-bending visitors have admitted that when they break a promise in this room, they are punished in swift and mysterious ways, such as a hard pinch on the leg or even

being lifted off the bed! Maybe Benjamin is acting up. Or maybe his mother, Sarah, insists all who visit her beloved son's room show good and respectful behavior?

Lucy's room thankfully features happier hauntings, such as the sounds of children playing or the voices of adults celebrating. Perhaps this is the ghostly imprint of the many weddings and family celebrations Lucy attended when she lived here. Her room is also where much of the ghostly mischief occurs. Spend a minute in the adjoining bathroom and you just might find the furniture rearranged when you return! Some guests have found a table or chair has moved clear across the room while they were just steps away behind the bathroom door. Members of one ghost tour even found themselves blocked from entering the room! A table seemed to have moved itself in front of the door. You may feel a happy energy in Lucy's room, but she will keep you on your toes!

The one room where spirits seem to have created a purely peaceful, loving atmosphere is the one named after Sarah, the mother of the house. People who have stayed in Sarah's room over the years report feeling looked after by a caring, maternal presence. Some wonder if Sarah's loving spirit was so strong in life it simply stuck around, mothering visitors long after her death.

Whether their night featured eerie paintings, a pinch on the leg, or just a good night's sleep, visitors to this mansion have long recorded their experiences in a guest book in the living room. If you go to Whitehall, you can read them yourself: tales of ghostly shadows, paranormal parties, and much more.

And, if you want to pay your respects to the Woodbridges and their family and friends, you can visit the Whitehall Cemetery nearby. The cemetery has a spookiness all its own . . . but at least there you can be pretty sure everyone will stay where they belong!

Mystic River

1784 Denison Home

BUILT 1784

Did Michael Cardillo know what he was in for when he first bought the lovely, historic Old Mystic Inn on Main Street (known today as the 1784 Denison Home)?" Maybe not, but he found out pretty quickly! It was a chilly December, and Michael's first order of business was to stack firewood outside the house, planning for cozy fires for the holidays. After a hard day's work, he settled into bed, imagining how wonderful it would be to welcome guests as the new innkeeper. He pictured guests from all walks of life filling the house, reading by the fireplaces, and soaking up the warm hospitality of his inn. In fact, his first guest had already arrived! His mother was staying in a bedroom right down the hall.

However, what Michael did *not* imagine at his inn were guests from all walks of AFTER-life! In the middle of the night, Michael's mother

woke to the sound of screaming. It sounded like Michael was truly terrified! She rushed to help and woke him from what she thought was an awful nightmare. Stunned and confused, Michael told her about his unsettling dream. He had seen a woman standing by the woodpile outside the house. She wore an old-fashioned white dress and stared intently at him—her eyes so piercing, he couldn't help but stare back. The woman didn't speak a word, but he could tell she was trying to communicate. Somehow, without making a sound, he felt her message loud and clear: "*Welcome to my home.*"

That was the first of many ghostly experiences.

The 1784 Denison Home is located in the hamlet of Old Mystic, the oldest part of town. This neighborhood is known to have more than its fair share of ghosts, and the home and property it sits on are no exception. At one time, the inn's immediate surroundings included Mystic's first schoolhouse (lost to fire in the 1900s) as well as its second. It has since been replaced by a children's playground, located right behind the inn. To this day, young spirits seem to gather there even after the park has emptied. Visitors at the inn report hearing echoes of children laughing and playing. Perhaps they're schoolchildren from days gone by, back to enjoy an eternal recess.

In 1959, the schoolhouse became The Old Mystic Book Shop, boasting "20,000 books." Customers remember the ground-floor rooms so filled with books that they could barely squeeze through! But Charles Vincent, the owner at the time, knew his inventory so well he could find any title with ease. (No wonder

all eight guest rooms are named after New England authors!) Today, Charles is still around in one way. An image of him—book in hand—is carved into the wooden sign that now hangs in front of the inn. (Some people say they've even seen the very same man reading in the gazebo.)

The building served as an inn before Michael bought it, but he hoped to make it even more special. Michael was a chef trained at the prestigious Culinary Institute of America. He looked forward to treating his guests to excellent meals as well as comfortable accommodations. He brought in his friend Robert to assist in the food preparation. In the early hours each morning, they started work on a day of gourmet meals.

One morning, as the two prepared breakfast, Robert thought he saw another person in the kitchen. *Surely not at this hour,* he told himself. No one else in the house would even be awake! But as he walked toward the counter where Michael was measuring ingredients, he stopped in shock: There, leaning over the counter directly across from Michael, was the ghostly figure of a woman in a long dress. From

her body language, she didn't seem to want to scare him or do any harm. On the contrary, she appeared to be closely supervising Michael's work—maybe even wishing she could get involved herself! Robert was amazed. But the strangest thing was that Michael hadn't seen her. Later, when Robert told Michael about the ghost, he didn't seem surprised or alarmed. Instead, Michael wondered if it was the same woman whose spooky welcome had given him such a shock in his dream.

Michael had grown used to strange noises in and around the house. He had also grown a bit more comfortable with the idea of sharing the inn with those who weren't ready to let it go. He really wanted to know more about this woman and her connection to the Old Mystic Inn. He called a psychic consultant to come to the house and tell him more about its restless spirits. What would the spirits have to say?

Did they have some deep, or fascinating, or maybe even terrifying message for him from the beyond?

To his relief, the ghost's message wasn't scary. In fact, it even made him smile. "Her name begins with *H*," the psychic told him, focusing hard. "And she has a message for you: *Use more fresh herbs and spices. And grate nutmeg over the eggnog!*" The psychic went on to relay a list of culinary critiques from the ghost. Then, with great concentration, the psychic learned a bit more about her story.

In colonial times, H had lived in the house and enjoyed cooking in the kitchen. Her loved one left, expecting to return, but never did. It was possible, H supposed, that he had drowned in the river, but she was waiting there just in case he came back to her. She ended her message with one more practical note: "*Please put a chair for me at the kitchen table*." Michael did. To this day, he expects she sits there watching while he cooks, trying to remind him about the fresh herbs and spices.

The psychic walked through the rest of the house and found more spirits: A clam farmer who had died in the house brought a sad, melancholy feeling wherever he roamed. A playful eight-year-old girl named Hannah may have lived in the house in the 1800s. As a ghost, she still liked to play one of her favorite games: hoop-trundling. In this game, a child guides a hoop along the ground with the use of a stick. Sometimes, guests hear her rolling hoop. Her other favorite pastime is sitting on her stool, playing around until she falls off and knocks it over! Others have felt the presence of a young boy in the house.

It's believed he drowned in a nearby brook. Even darker is the story of two voices near the playground: One cries, "*Help me! Help me!*" The other answers, "*No.*"

Thankfully, most of the spirits at the 1784 Denison Home seem friendly and content to be in such a busy, beautiful place. Psychics and paranormal researchers love to visit this ghost-filled house. Occasionally, they'll catch snippets of everyday ghostly conversations: "*I thought Nathan was here.*" "*That's a vehicle.*" "*Are you a policeman?*" Sometimes when they first arrive, they'll hear a charming welcome: "*Come on in!*"

Once, Michael and Robert were working downstairs. The only guest at the inn that day had gone out, but they heard footsteps upstairs. They assumed the guest had returned. Imagine their surprise when later, she walked in the front door! By then, however, they were becoming accustomed to supernatural happenings. Many guests had told them about a woman in white seen walking through the inn—the same woman, Michael felt certain, who'd been in his dream. A neighbor suggested she might be Margaret Dart, a young woman who had died in a fire nearby. Were these footsteps also from Margaret? The woman in white? H, the avid cook? Nathan? Or maybe Hannah?

This long roster of spirits was probably not exactly what Michael expected when he bought the inn. Then again, he *did* get one of his wishes: a full house!

Mystic, Connecticut

Factory Square

BUILT 1850s

While shipbuilding and the sea trade were long the main industries in Mystic, they weren't the only ones. During the days when Factory Square housed a working factory, it made a variety of products. At one time, the workers here manufactured cotton gins, machines for removing seeds from cotton plants. Later, the factory produced book-binding equipment, and at another point, it produced engines for boats. But did you know that factories also make for great *ghost stories*?

Mystic's Factory Square is no exception.

In the 1800s and early 1900s, hundreds of people worked here every day. In fact, many of them spent more of their time on this site than in their own homes. All that human energy— all those life stories coming together—tends to leave a mark on a place. This impact may have been even stronger because of the risk involved. Factory work was dangerous. There were machines hot enough to melt metal, clamps and stamps that could slam down hard enough to crush a person, fast-moving cutters and pokers and pins. That is to say: Beyond spending so much of their lives here, it is likely multiple people met their *deaths* here, too.

Today, those industrial dangers are gone from Factory Square. Instead, the large brick building has been renovated. It's home to restaurants, offices, and condominium apartments. It's a place designed to be inviting to modern *living* people. However, not all the long-dead factory workers seem to have gotten the news! For many years, a restaurant called Voodoo Grill operated here. Though it's no longer open today, this spot became a particular favorite haunt.

Voodoo Grill had an interesting mix of "residual hauntings" and "active hauntings." Residual hauntings are the type where people see or sense a ghostly presence, but the ghost doesn't seem to be aware of the modern world. It's as if a video was taken during their lifetime, and now it is just replaying over and over. In active hauntings, the ghost is aware of living people. It may even try to help, or scare, or talk to them. It may move physical objects. Think of a ghost girl playing hide-and-seek with a new friend, or a spirit who gives cooking advice. Those are active hauntings. Think you can tell the difference? Here are five mini-ghost stories from Voodoo Grill. See if you can tell which kind is which!

1. CRASH-DOWN

Joe is early for dinner with a friend, so he finds a seat at the bar to wait for her. After a few minutes, he finds himself staring mindlessly at the rack of wine glasses above the bar. He counts the rows just for something to do. Then, a sudden change in the light draws his attention to one glass in particular. It's as if it has moved, ever so slightly, completely on its own. Joe stares, transfixed, as the glass moves forward a little more, then a little more, until it is almost to the end of the rack. *The rack must be slanted downward,* Joe tells himself, *and the glass is just being tugged downward by gravity.* That makes some sense. But what happens next makes no sense at all.

With no human hand nearby, the glass comes forward out of the rack but does not fall. Instead, it hovers in the air for a few seconds.

Not everyone in the bar has noticed. But they notice what happens next. The glass plunges to the floor, filling the whole room with the sound of glass shattering. It sounds like the breaking of not one, but *one hundred* wine glasses! The bartender rushes to see what has happened, but when she looks at the floor, all she sees is the single broken wine glass, split cleanly in two.

2. AFTER HOURS

Frank the janitor doesn't get ruffled by much. He knows some of the staff members have been spooked by weird noises or seen objects fall when they shouldn't. One person even claimed to see a floating fork! Frank himself has heard footsteps in the bathroom when he knows for a fact no one is there. But even that doesn't worry him. It's a good thing he's so calm. His shift is in the middle of the night, an hour or more past closing time.

Frank works alone as he gives the bar and dining room a thorough cleaning. One night, he's polishing the mirror behind the bar when he catches sight of an odd reflection in the glass. It looks like there are people sitting around one of the tables! He calls out, "Bar's closed!" and turns around to tell the group to leave. But as soon as he does, they seem to disappear. Confused, Frank turns back to the mirror and there they are again. Several men, all wearing factory uniforms from the 1920s or 30s, are sitting around a table in the middle of the eerily quiet room. They're completely ignoring him. Frank spins around to face the room. Once more, the group has vanished. Now they have disappeared from both the real room *and* the reflection. Frank finishes scrubbing the bar and prepares to leave. But the sound of old-fashioned music stops him in his tracks. It's "big band" jazz from the 1920s. He goes to turn off the stereo but finds it already off! Determined, he unplugs the stereo. But even *that* doesn't have an effect. The music plays for another few minutes, then finally fades away.

3. Spill-Proof

On a shelf behind the bar, there's a long row of bottles, each containing a different type of liquor. The bartender takes a customer's order, then lifts the bottle of gin from its slot to mix the cocktail the customer has requested. When she's done pouring, the bartender puts the bottle back in its place and turns to the sink to wash the cocktail shaker. But suddenly, a sound like a gunshot rings out through the restaurant. *BANG!* Startled customers and staff members look quickly around to see what happened. Those looking toward the bar see it first: One by one, like a row of dominoes, the bottles on the shelf have begun to tip and fall to the floor. *BANG! BANG! BANG!* The bartender and other staff members survey the damage. All the bottles that sat on a high shelf just moments before are on the floor. But somehow, not even one has broken!

Mystified, the group begins to pick them up one at a time, carefully replacing them on the shelf. The last bottle the bartender picks up

happens to be the bottle of gin. Only now, there appears to be a *bullet hole* straight through it. She stares at the bottle, baffled. Not a drop was spilled! Speculation starts to swirl about what could have caused the strange event. Some locals remember a rumor about the plot of land the factory was built on. They say it was once a public square where executions may have taken place. Could this be a ghostly member of a firing squad taking one last shot from beyond the grave? Or maybe even the victim . . . finally shooting back?

4. Mopping Up

The restaurant has closed for the night and it's time to prepare for the next day, so Rachel goes to the upstairs supply room to get cleaning supplies: cleaning spray, sponge, broom, mop. But on her way back downstairs, she realizes she left something behind. "Whoops!" she exclaims. "Forgot the bucket." She turns and starts to head back up but freezes, astonished by what she sees. On the second-floor landing, someone has placed a dozen or more buckets neatly in a line, as if displayed for her to choose from. Feeling a chill dart up her spine, Rachel grabs the closest one, races back downstairs, and calls to the manager to show him what happened. The manager is equally amazed: Not only is he clueless how the buckets got there . . . he didn't know the restaurant even *had* that many buckets to begin with!

5. A TO B

In another part of Factory Square, not far from where Voodoo Grill was once located, the building was renovated into a stylish living space with all the modern features. A new tenant who recently moved in has a completely up-to-date unit. Well, *almost*. From time to time, while the tenant is working, cooking, or just watching TV, a ghostly figure walks by. Wearing an old-fashioned factory uniform,

the figure casually walks from one point to the next—often vanishing through solid walls! The man appears relaxed but determined as he moves back and forth through the apartment, paying no attention to the divisions that now stand where there must have once been open space. He never seems to notice modern earthly details like brick and concrete—or even the shaken tenant himself. A tenant whose new apartment has one ghostly feature he *definitely* didn't expect.

RESIDUAL OR ACTIVE HAUNTINGS?

ANSWERS

Did you spot the difference? Here are the categories that match each story:

1. Crash-Down: *Active Haunting*

It's not clear who moved the glass or why. But since the force moved an object in the physical world (and in a way that didn't make physical sense), this was an active haunting.

2. After Hours: *Residual Haunting*

Frank witnessed a rare residual haunting. The people in the reflection seemed completely unaware of him.

3. Spill-Proof: *Undetermined*

There are different theories on this one. Since it affected physical objects, it appears to be an active haunting. On the other hand, it is possible that noise from a residual haunting could be loud enough to cause physical damage. (Tricky, right?)

4. Mopping Up: *Active Haunting*

Not only did the ghostly presence in this story move physical objects (the buckets), but it also responded directly to Rachel's situation, showing awareness of its modern-day surroundings.

5. A to B: *Residual Haunting*

The apartment ghost is a classic residual haunting. The ghost follows the repetitive patterns of a long-ago routine without any awareness of the present-day world. The new layout of the space doesn't fit those routines anymore, but he doesn't seem to realize it. And as long as he can walk through walls, he probably won't notice all the updates to the building—or even, that he's a ghost.

CHAPTER 6

The Emporium Building

BUILT 1859

You don't have to be psychic or even especially sensitive to pick up otherworldly vibes at this *super-spooky* Water Street building. Over the decades, the Emporium Building has played many roles, serving as a general store, post office, war office, hotel, restaurant, and art gallery—and seems to have picked up at least one or two ghosts for every era in its history. In fact, when Courtney McInvale—Mystic's resident "Ghost Lady" tour guide—shows her tour groups the town's most haunted sites, this is one location they don't need her to point out. *"That one is definitely haunted!"* *"Are we learning about this one?"* Guest after guest feels strangely drawn to the building, convinced there are spirits within.

Yes, this one is most certainly believed to be haunted. And yes—let's learn about it!

There may be many ghostly beings haunting this historic building, but there are three stars of the show: one upstairs and two downstairs. The second floor is the domain of a female spirit called, fittingly, "the Lady Upstairs." Frequently seen peering out of upstairs windows, the Lady appears formal—even prim—in her appearance. Her hair is in a tight bun and her feet in high-heel shoes. Although some see the Lady as a protector, standing guard over the Emporium Building, most who encounter her find their meeting memorably chilling.

In one notable account from the 1960s, an owner of the building was painting floorboards upstairs. He was about to open the space as The Emporium, a variety store selling knick-knacks, candy, antiques, and more. With just a couple of weeks until the grand opening, the anxious owner was working fast. He realized too late that he had painted himself into a corner! If he wanted to preserve the paint job, he had no choice but to wait for the paint to dry.

While he waited, he heard high heels slowly walking across the wood floors downstairs. He thought a customer must have wandered in, not realizing the store was closed. "We're closed!" he called downstairs. But the footsteps continued across the floor. "I'm sorry," he called again, "I need to ask you to leave!" Then, to his shock, the footsteps began climbing the stairs. They seemed to approach the room

he had just painted, though he couldn't see anyone connected to the sound. And then, to his astonishment, the footsteps walked right into the room! The owner watched, scared out of his wits, as an invisible lady left *very* visible footprints in the still-wet paint, marking her path from the open doorway straight into the opposite wall—where they suddenly disappeared!

Luckily, the *downstairs* ghosts of 15 Water Street have a friendlier reputation. As with the Lady Upstairs, no one is exactly sure how or why they are connected to the building. But these two young spirits never seem shy about showing up. Most people who have spotted them have just assumed they were ordinary boys at play. Back when The Emporium was open, customers so frequently asked staff members about the boys' identities, the staff eventually gave them names so they could answer simply, without causing alarm. Answering, "*Who? I don't see any boys there!*" tended to give people chills and send them running. Instead, staff members just said, "*Oh, that's just Willy and Billy. They love to come in and play.*"

It is possible spirits from the much more distant past still linger here, too. After all, there's been a building here ever since the early 1700s. Before that, the Pequots used this place as a temporary shelter or sanctuary during times of war. During the Civil War, the building was used as a war office where soldiers came to enlist. Family members (perhaps even the Lady Upstairs) also came to learn the fate of their loved ones on the battlefield. For both the Pequots and the Union soldiers, this place was a key piece of a war story—as lived by real people under great stress. Those feelings and experiences surely left an imprint on the property.

Today, 15 Water Street is the home of the Mystic Museum of Arts, where visitors can take in many aspects of Mystic history at once: the beautiful riverfront, inspiring local artists, and possibly even a ghost (or three!).

CHAPTER 7

Anthony J's Bistro and The Mariner

BUILT 1844 AND 1974

In the mood for seafood? Head to The Mariner for dinner! Feeling more like pasta? You can't do much better than Anthony J's. Hoping to spot some haunted happenings during your meal? Either one of these sister restaurants is sure to hit the spot. Anthony J (Anthony J. Torraca, though his friends call him "Skip") is the owner of both famously haunted Mystic eateries. People love the food, but it's Skip's tradition of warm hospitality that keeps the regulars coming back ... and sometimes staying a bit longer than you'd think.

Each of Skip's restaurants has its signature cuisine, décor, *and* a signature ghost. At Anthony J's, the cuisine is Italian. The décor is sentimental, featuring photos of friends who have passed away. And the ghost ... is Richard. During his lifetime, Rich loved Anthony J's. He praised almost everything about it: the food, the wine, the ambiance, the staff. The one thing that drove Rich crazy about Anthony J's was the way Skip decorated the place for the holidays: Big, shiny Christmas ornaments hung all over the restaurant. Year after year, this brought on a flood of outrage from Rich. *They were so tacky!* he protested. After a while, Rich's outrage became something of its own holiday tradition, with Skip laughing affectionately (and stubbornly refusing to give up the giant Christmas baubles).

One autumn, after many happy years, Rich passed away. Skip hung his picture on the Anthony J's wall of honor. When the holidays rolled around again, staff members felt bittersweet pulling the Christmas ornaments out of storage. The thing that had so enraged Rich now seemed so connected to him! As they took the decorations out of the boxes, the staff smiled, warmly remembering their friend. They counted and then counted again, but there was no denying it: One of the biggest, boldest ornaments was gone! They searched their homes and storage units, but it was truly nowhere to be found. They had to admit, Rich had finally gotten his way!

Months passed, and they forgot all about the lost ornament. Then one warm July morning, the staff arrived for their shifts to find a surprise waiting for them. There, in the middle of the floor, was the missing Christmas ornament! If there had ever been any doubt who was behind the prank, there wasn't anymore. *"Richard!"* the group whispered in amazement.

The Mariner has its own secret sauce to haunted-restaurant success. It offers surf-and-turf dinners, and a nautical atmosphere highlighted by the six hundred oars hanging on the walls alongside pieces of historic ships. There's also a ghost named John, who looks like he just might stick around forever. When John retired from his career as a federal agent, he eagerly took up a new role: beloved regular at the restaurant of his lifelong friend, Skip. John could often be found sitting on his favorite barstool at The Mariner, chatting with Skip and joking with the waiters and bartenders. The staff members quickly became dear friends, too.

When John died a few years after his retirement, his picture was hung behind the bar across from his usual spot. The staff saw it as a fitting tribute as they said farewell to their companion. But John wasn't quite ready for goodbyes *just yet*.

One morning, soon after John's death, the owners came in to find odd changes to the décor. A couple of the oars on the wall had been turned upside-down. A single photograph on the wall was askew: John's. A couple of days later, they arrived to find a few more of the oars facing opposite from their usual positions.

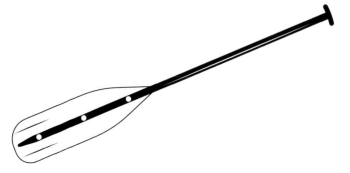

Once again, John's picture was askew. The pattern was starting to look deliberate. Could it be a message from beyond? Maybe from John *himself*?

That same night, it seemed they had an answer. After closing the restaurant, the staff did their usual cleanup, stacking the chairs and placing each barstool on top of the bar before they walked to the door to leave. But on this night, something made them pause and take one last look at the bar. When they did, they saw a sign that seemed impossible to ignore. One barstool had moved from the bar top back to its place on the floor. It was, of course, John's favorite seat—a message to one and all that this Mariner regular was still with them, in his own mischievous way.

Legends of
Mystic River

In an old coastal town brimming with history, family lore, and homes dating back to colonial times, it's no wonder many of Mystic's most famous ghost stories are attached to specific homes or buildings. But some of Mystic's spookiest tales aren't contained within specific walls. They're in the wilds and waters of Mystic itself.

Back in the 1970s, a creature called the "Pigman" was said to terrorize Vermont teens who strayed into the woods at night. The teens described a man's body with a pig's face and hooves—definitely a frightful figure to meet late at night! A decade later, tales of a "Mystic Pigman" emerged: a creature with a human-like body but a very *un*-human face, with a snout and beady eyes. The creature

had an angry, snorting call. Some Mystic high school boys claimed to have spotted him one night in the midst of a bizarre and frightening scene. The boys said they were walking along Holmes Street when the sounds of a woman's screams drew them toward the riverfront. They ran to the scene. When they arrived,

they saw what looked like a man about to push the frightened woman into the river! The boys shouted for him to stop. To their horror, he lifted the woman up and threw her into the Mystic. She sank out of sight, never to re-emerge. The figure then turned to the boys. They saw his grotesque features clearly for the first time. They froze in their tracks, terrified. He made a screeching-snort sound, dove into the water, and disappeared, just as she had.

Some thought the boys' story must have had a kernel of truth, since they were known to be bullies at school. Why would they make up a story that cast them as the weaker side of a fight? Around the same time, a police report revealed that a local woman had gone missing. She was never found. Perhaps she was the Pigman's unfortunate victim?

Most of Mystic's outdoor hauntings come not from the woods, but from the water. People who live near the sea know its gifts and dangers. For hundreds of years, ocean waters have nourished Mystic, offering jobs to fishermen (and, long ago, whalers), boatbuilders, and shippers of goods.

Much of this history can be seen at Mystic Seaport. Here, historic crafts like the nineteenth-century whaling ship *Charles W. Morgan*—the last of its kind—have become a familiar sight to locals. Sadly, accidents at sea were even more common in the days of the *Morgan* and its fleet. Forecasting and tracking technologies were much less developed then. Watching a loved one sail out of safe harbor could feel like sending them into battle. Wives and families hoped for a victorious return but knew that each trip could be the last. This anxiety lies beneath some of the most haunting legends of Mystic River—especially its infamous ghost ships.

One such ship appears to depart from Mystic Seaport, heading slowly downriver toward the drawbridge and Long Island Sound. To those watching it go by, it looks old enough to be the *Charles W. Morgan* itself. But that doesn't seem quite right. For one thing, it is smaller in size. For another, there appears to be no crew in sight! As the ship approaches the drawbridge, spectators wait for the bells and flashing lights that mean the bridge is about to lift to let a ship pass. But when the ship is *this* ship, the bridge doesn't open. Some people watching must know what is coming. But others start to panic as the boat maintains its steady speed toward the bridge. Just when a crash seems unavoidable, the ship disappears! Was this the shadow of a long-ago boat on its way to an ill-fated journey? No one knows for sure. But it is a solemn reminder of the perils of a seafaring life.

People report seeing another ghostly craft from time to time. A boat floats down the river, carrying a single, motionless sailor at the front. It stops briefly before carrying on down the waterway and disappearing. Those who have seen it say that the sailor is a crew member who was lost at sea, now recreating his fateful departure—or perhaps seeking the safe harbor he couldn't reach in life.

The lost seaman trying to connect with home is a common thread in Mystic lore. One of the best known of these stories takes place on a stormy night in 1875. While her husband-to-be was out to sea aboard the fishing ship *Commodore*, a young woman named Lydia sat with her family, planning her longed-for wedding. Despite the terrible weather, the women seemed cozy and hopeful as they chatted around the fireplace.

But then, the tiniest omen began to set the bride on edge. A drop of rain fell down the chimney, sizzling instantly to nothing. Lydia looked toward the window and saw a much, much worse omen. There, as though reflected in the pane of glass, was her fiancé. But instead of the handsome smile and rosy cheeks she knew, he appeared grim and wan like a corpse. As she saw him, the engagement ring slipped from her finger and broke in two. Despite this chorus of bad omens, Lydia tried to quiet her fears. After all, she always felt nervous when her love was away at sea. He had always come back before.

There was no reason to believe he wouldn't return safely.

The next morning, however, the signs were verified by the awful truth. Lydia received word that her fiancé had washed overboard and drowned. It was an awful revelation that somehow, already, she knew. She is just one of the many wives and sweethearts of Mystic sailors who never returned from sea.

The Mystic Drawbridge

"The Morgan" in Mystic Seaport

A Ghostly Goodbye

The spooky tales of Mystic start with fire and end with water—a fitting cycle for a town on the edge of land and sea, of past and present, and even of ordinary life and the spirit world beyond. It's an intersection full of contrast and mystery, but also of possibility.

When you next walk past a Mystic building and feel a little chill, peek at the upstairs windows. You may see a nodding head with

a tidy bun. A young girl gazing out to sea. Or
even a window slowly opening and closing on
its own. In your own home, you may sense a
guiding hand as you try a new recipe in the

kitchen, or hear footsteps or old-fashioned music from an unknown source. We hope you'll be inspired by these tales of haunted Mystic to open your senses to the unexpected. You may decide that some of what you hear is only your imagination ... but tune in closely, and you just might discover something truly *mystical!*

Beth Landis Hester is originally from the haunted city of New Orleans, where she sometimes heard ghostly footsteps in the very old house where she grew up . . . and awoke one morning to find a mysterious footprint on her ceiling! These days, she lives in New England with her husband, two children, and one spooky dog, and (most of) the footprints stay on the floor. You can find her at bethhester.com.

Check out some of the other *Spooky America* titles available now!

Spooky America was adapted from the creeptastic *Haunted America* series for adults. *Haunted America* explores historical haunts in cities and regions across America. Here's more from the original *Haunted Mystic* author Courtney McInvale:

www.courtneymcinvale.com
www.seasideshadows.com